KETO COOKBOOK FOR

CARB LOVERS

Feed Your Carbs Cravings With 40+
Delicious, And Simple Carbs Related
Ketogenic Recipes to Melt Off Fat Quickly. Do
not Miss The Keto Cookbook For Carbs Lovers
of Any Age or Gender.

Table of Contents

INTRODUCTION

A ketogenic diet is a low-fat, low-carb diet intended to help fat digestion. At the point when the body runs out of glucose stores, it changes to utilizing fat and unsaturated fats, which produce intensifies called ketones. Ketones cross the blood-cerebrum boundary and enter the mind, where they are utilized as an elective fuel source. Basically, it is an eating routine that makes the body discharge ketones into the circulation system. Most cells like to utilize glucose, which comes from sugars, as the body's fundamental wellspring of energy. Since it needs carbs, a ketogenic diet is wealthy in proteins and fats. It ordinarily incorporates a lot of meats, eggs, prepared meats, wieners, cheeses, fish, nuts, spread, oils, seeds, and sinewy vegetables. Cyclical ketogenic diets are more advanced methods and primarily used by bodybuilders or athletes. Carbs are the fundamental wellspring of energy for our body. Without enough carbs for energy, the body separates fat into ketones. The ketones at that point become the essential wellspring of fuel for the body. Ketones give energy to the heart, kidneys and different muscles. The body additionally utilizes ketones as an elective fuel hotspot for the mind. As on a Keto diet, carbs from all sources are seriously limited so it becomes difficult for carb lovers to maintain Keto diet and follow the Keto diet schedule.

One of the biggest challenges of following the ketogenic diet is swearing off favorite foods that are high in carbs (think sweets, mashed potatoes, and bread). "Low-carb and Keto diet plans often require a lot of meal prep and planning, since the majority of prepackaged foods are more processed and higher in carbohydrates. This book contains recipes especially for carb lovers who want to adopt Keto diet and also get the taste of high carb meals.

1. Keto Pecan Crescent Cookies

YIELDS: 20| PREP TIME: 0 HOURS 20 MINS |

TOTAL TIME: 1 HOUR 5 MINS

INGREDIENTS

FOR THE COOKIES

- 2 c. almond flour
- 1 c. finely chopped walnuts
- 2 tbsp. coconut flour
- 1/2 tsp. preparing powder
- 1/4 tsp. genuine salt
- 1/2 c. (1 stick) spread, mellowed

- 2/3 c. Turn brown sugar (or ordinary Swerve and 2 tsp. Yacon syrup)
- 1 large egg
- 1/2 tsp. unadulterated vanilla concentrate

FOR THE VANILLA GLAZE

- 2/3 c. powdered Swerve sugar or powdered erythritol
- 6 to 8 tbsp. hefty cream
- 1/2 tsp. unadulterated vanilla concentrate

DIRECTIONS
FOR THE COOKIES

1. Preheat oven to 325° and fix 2 preparing sheets with material paper. In a medium bowl, whisk together almond flour, chopped walnuts, coconut flour, heating powder, and salt.
2. In a large bowl, beat spread with Swerve until light and feathery, around 2 minutes. Beat in egg and vanilla concentrate. Beat in almond flour combination until mixture meets up.
3. Structure batter into 3/4", at that point fold among palms and shape into bows. Spot on arranged preparing sheets.
4. Prepare 15 to 18 minutes, or until just softly brilliant brown. They won't be firm to the

touch, yet will solidify as they cool. Cool on the sheets.

FOR THE GLAZE

1. Whisk powdered Swerve with 1/4 cup cream and vanilla concentrate until smooth. Add 1 tablespoon more cream at a time until a slight however spreadable consistency is accomplished.
2. Spread on cooled treats and brighten as wanted.
3. Then again, essentially move treats in powdered sugar.

2. Greek Yogurt Zucchini Bread

Prep time: 10 minutes Cooking time: 50

minutes Total time: 4 hours (including cooling)

Yield: 1 loaf

INGREDIENTS:

- 1/3 cup (80 ml) canola, vegetable, or melted coconut oil
- 1/2 cup (120 ml) of organic blue agave
- 1 large egg, at room temperature
- 1/2 cup (121 g) Greek yogurt, at room temperature *
- 1 and 1/2 teaspoons of pure vanilla extract
- 1 and 1/2 cups (190 g) all-purpose flour (scoop and leveled)
- 1 teaspoon of baking powder

- 1/2 teaspoon of baking powder
- 1/2 teaspoon of salt
- 1 teaspoon of cinnamon powder
- 1 cup shredded zucchini (about 1 medium) *
- Optional: 2 teaspoons orange peel (so delicious!)
- optional: 3/4 cup (95 g) chopped walnuts, (115 g) raisins, or (135 g) chocolate chips

DIRECTIONS:

1. Preheat the oven to 350 ° F (177 ° C) and grease a 9 × 5-inch bread pan.
2. Beat the oil, agave, egg, yogurt, and vanilla together in a medium bowl until combined. In a large bowl, whisk together the flour, baking powder, baking powder, salt, and cinnamon. Pour the wet into the dry and mix with a large wooden spoon or rubber spatula until combined. Avoid over mixing. Fold in the zucchini, orange zest, and walnuts.

3. Divide the batter into the prepared bread pan. Bake for 40-50 minutes. Baking times vary, so keep an eye on yours. The bread is done when a toothpick inserted in the center comes out clean. If you notice that the top of the bread browns too quickly in the oven, cover it loosely with aluminum foil.

4. Remove the bread from the oven and place it on a wire rack. Let cool completely before slicing and serving—cover and store leftover bread at room temperature for up to 5 days.

3. Greek Yogurt Alfredo Sauce

Prep Time: 5 MINUTES Cooking Time: 5 MINUTES Total Time: 10 MINUTES Servings: 4

INGREDIENTS:

- Two-tablespoons butter
- 1 1/2 teaspoons garlic powder
- 1/2 cup milk or water (I used fat-free half & half)
- 3/4 cup plain Greek yogurt (I used 0% fat)
- 1/2 - 2/3 cup shredded parmesan cheese
- salt and pepper to taste
- optional: 1/2 teaspoon dried parsley (or one teaspoon fresh)

DIRECTIONS:

1. Melt the butter in a medium saucepan over medium heat. Stir in the garlic powder. Stir in the milk (or water). Remove from heat and let cool for 2-3 minutes. Gradually beat in Greek yogurt.

2. Add parmesan cheese to the sauce and stir until melted. (If the cheese doesn't melt completely because the sauce is too cold, put it on low heat for a few minutes) Add salt and pepper to taste and mix with your favorite cooked pasta noodles.

4. Healthy Greek Yogurt Lemon Parmesan Cheese Tilapia

Prep time: 10 minutes Cooking time: 10 minutes Yield:

INGREDIENTS:

- 4 (4 oz.) filets tilapia fresh or thawed if frozen
- 1/2 teaspoon salt plus more to taste
- 1/2 teaspoon pepper
- 2 tablespoons unsalted butter melted
- 2 tablespoons nonfat plain Greek yogurt
- 2 tablespoons lemon juice about 1 lemon juiced + more for serving
- 2 tablespoons grated parmesan cheese
- 1/2 teaspoon garlic powder
- 1/2 teaspoon dried Italian seasoning

- 1/4 teaspoon red pepper flakes omit if you don't like spice, a little goes a long way in this recipe

DIRECTIONS:

1. Preheat oven to 400 degrees F and grease a 9x13 inch baking dish with cooking spray.
2. Dry tilapia thoroughly with kitchen paper
3. Place in the prepared baking dish.
4. Sprinkle tilapia with salt and pepper.
5. Put aside.
6. In a small bowl, stir together melted butter, Greek yogurt, lemon juice, Parmesan, garlic powder, Italian herbs, and red pepper flakes.
7. Spoon the butter mixture evenly over the tilapia fillets.
8. Bake in the preheated oven for 10-12 minutes, or until the tilapia is cooked through and peeling off easily with a fork.
9. Serve with more salt and lemon juice to taste.

5. American-style sugar-free scones

INGREDIENTS:

- 2 cups of almond flour
- 1/3 cup of Erythritol
- 2-teaspoons of baking powder
- ¼ cup of unsalted butter melted
- 1-teaspoon Vanilla Essence
- 1-large egg
- Icing ingredients:
- ½ cup of Sukrin Melis
- 1-2 tablespoons of unsweetened almond milk
- ½ teaspoon of vanilla essence

DIRECTIONS:

1. Preheat the oven to 175C / 350F. Cover a baking tray with parchment paper. In a mixing bowl, add the almond flour, Erythritol, and baking powder. Mix well.

2. Add the unsalted butter, vanilla, and eggs and mix into thick dough. Roll the dough into a ball and press it into a disk on the prepared baking sheet.

3. Cut into six wedges and carefully separate them. Bake for 20-25 minutes, until golden brown.

4. Let cool for 15 minutes. For the icing, add the sukrin melis and vanilla essence to a small bowl and beat; slowly add the almond milk until thick and pourable. Drizzle the icing over the cooled scones, and enjoy!

6. Keto Bagels Recipe

INGREDIENTS:

- 2-teaspoons of dried yeast
- 1-teaspoon of inulin
- 2-tablespoons of warm water
- 10 ounces of mozzarella shredded
- 2-tablespoons of butter melted
- 6 ounces of almond flour
- 2-teaspoons of baking powder
- 1-teaspoon of xanthan gum
- 3-large eggs one is for egg washing
- 2-tablespoons of everything season

DIRECTIONS:

1. In a large mixing bowl, add the yeast, inulin, and warm water and set aside to rise. Melt the mozzarella and butter until completely melted. This can be done in the microwave or a saucepan on the stove. When the yeast is frothy, add the almond flour, baking powder, and xanthan gum and mix well. Pour over the hot melted cheese mixture and toss into the almond flour mixture; about halfway through the mix, add 2 of the eggs.

2. Keep mixing until you have slightly sticky dough. I highly recommend mixing the dough with gloved hands for the best results. Set the dough aside and make a large baking tray by lining it with parchment paper.

3. Set your oven to 180C / 355F. Divide your dough into eight pieces of equal size. Ours weighed between 75-80g and 2.6-2.8oz. Roll each piece of dough into a ball and run your finger through the center to make an opening.

4. To make the opening wider, gently twist the dough around your finger as if it were a small hula hoop. Place your bagel on the parchment-lined baking sheet and repeat Step 8 for the remaining dough pieces.

5. Break the extra egg into a small bowl and beat well. Divide your Everything Seasoning on a plate ready for dipping.

6. Gently brush each bagel with an egg wash, and then press them into the spices.

7. Return it to the baking sheet and move on to the other bagel. When all the bagels are seasoned, let them stand in a warm place for 15 minutes to rise.

8. Bake in the oven for 15-20 minutes, until brown. Remove from oven and let cool 10 minutes before enjoying.

7. Keto Double Chocolate Muffins

CAL/SERV: 280 | YIELDS: 1 DOZEN | PREP TIME: 0 HOURS 10 MINS | TOTAL TIME: 0 HOURS 25 MINS

INGREDIENTS

- 2 c. almond flour
- 3/4 c. unsweetened cocoa powder
- 1/4 c. turn sugar
- 1/2 tsp. preparing powder
- 1 tsp. legitimate salt
- 1 c. (2 sticks) spread, liquefied
- 3 large eggs
- 1 tsp. unadulterated vanilla concentrate

- 1 c. without sugar dim chocolate chips, like Lily's

DIRECTIONS

1. Preheat oven to 350° and fix a biscuit tin with liners. In a large bowl whisk together almond flour, cocoa powder, Swerve, preparing powder, and salt. Add liquefied spread, eggs, and vanilla and mix until joined.
2. Overlap in chocolate chips.
3. Split player between biscuit liners and prepare until a toothpick embedded into the center tells the truth, 12 minutes.

8. Sugar Free Chocolate Bark with Bacon and Almonds

Prep Time: 30 minutes | Cook Time: 0 minutes

| Total Time: 30 minutes | Servings: 8

INGREDIENTS

- 1 9 oz. pack Sugar free Chocolate Chips
- 1/2 cup Chopped Almonds
- 2 cuts bacon cooked and disintegrated

Guidelines

1. In a microwave safe bowl, microwave the chocolate chips on high for 30 seconds, mix. Microwave for 30 additional seconds and mix. Microwave for 15 seconds at that point mix one final time. You need to ensure you have a smidgen of unmelted chocolate chips extra when you haul it out of the microwave. At that

point mix one final time and it ought to be totally liquefied.

2. add the chopped almonds to the softened chocolate and mix
3. On a material lined heating sheet, pour the chocolate blend in a meager layer, around 1/2 inch.
4. Sprinkle the disintegrated bacon on top of the chocolate and press in with a spatula.
5. Refrigerate for 20 minutes or until the chocolate has totally solidified. Strip the material from the chocolate and break into 8 pieces. Store in the fridge.

- For 1/8 of recipe: 157 cal
- 12.8g fat
- 12.7g carbs
- 7.5g fiber
- 4g protein

9. Broccoli And Bacon Croquettes

Preparation Time: 20 min |Chilling Time: 20 min |Total Time: 1 hour| Servings: 14 Croquettes | Calories: 126kcal

INGREDIENTS:

- 1 pound of broccoli
- 2 oz. butter
- 3 slices of bacon
- 1/2 cup of grated parmesan cheese
- 1 egg
- 2 oz. pork rinds crushed into crumbs
- 1 teaspoon of salt
- 2 teaspoons of pepper
- 1 tbsp. Linseed ground
- 1 tbsp. almond flour

DIRECTIONS:

1. Boil or steam broccoli for 5 minutes or until tender, drain well.

2. Mix the warm broccoli with the butter into a puree. Place in a bowl and stir in the grated Parmesan cheese, pepper and salt.

3. Cut the bacon into small pieces and cook over low to medium heat for 6 to 8 minutes. The bacon fat will melt while the bacon is browning, add the bacon and fat to the broccoli and mix well.

4. Chill the broccoli and bacon mixture for at least 30 minutes.

5. Set your fryer to 350F / 180C and let it heat up.

6. After the mix has cooled, add the egg and ground pork rinds and mix well.

7. Roll the mixture into 14 small barrel molds.

8. On a plate, mix the almond flour and linseed flour, roll each croquette through this dry mixture, making sure each side is covered, then press the mixture onto the surface of the croquette.

9. Fry your croquettes in batches, so that you do not overfill the fryer. They will take about 3-5 minutes, remove when crispy and golden brown. To enjoy!

10. Delicious Vegetable Medley

INGREDIENTS:

- 6 tablespoons of olive oil
- 240 g baby Bella mushrooms
- 115 g broccoli
- 100 g sugar snaps
- 90 g paprika
- 90 g spinach
- 2 tablespoons of pumpkin seeds
- 2 teaspoons of chopped garlic
- 1 teaspoon of salt
- 1 teaspoon of pepper
- ½ teaspoon of red pepper flakes

DIRECTIONS:

1. Start cooking all of your vegetables. Cut the 115 g broccoli into bite-sized florets. Cut the 90 g bell pepper into strips and then finely chop the strips. If you're not using pre-sliced mushrooms, make sure to slice your 240g mushrooms in this too.

2. Add 6 tablespoons. Olive oil in a wok and bring to hot heat.

3. When the oil is hot, add garlic and let it cook for 1 minute.

4. Once the garlic starts to brown, add the mushrooms and stir to combine.

5. When the mushrooms have absorbed most of the oil, add the broccoli and mix well.

6. Add 100 g Sugar Snap Peas to the mixture and stir well.

7. Add your peppers to the bowl and stir well. You want the peppers to still be a little crunchy by the time you're done.

8. Add all your herbs: 1 tsp. Salt, 1 tsp. Pepper and 1/2 tsp. Red Pepper Flakes. Taste here and add more spices if desired.

9. Add 2 tablespoons. Pumpkin seeds and stirs them into the vegetables.

10. When the vegetables are cooked, place 90 g spinach on top of the vegetables and let the steam reduce them.

11. Once the spinach has shrunk, mix everything together and serve!

11. Keto Blueberry Lemon Cheesecake Bars

Yield: 12 | Prep Time: 20 Minutes | Cook Time: 20 Minutes | Total Time: 40 Minutes

Ingredients

Almond Flour Crust

- 8 tablespoons spread
- 1/4 cup almond flour
- 2 tablespoons turn sugar
- Low Carb Blueberry Sauce
- 1/2 cup blueberries
- 1/4 cup water
- 1/3 cup of confectioners turn sugar

Lemon Cheesecake Layer

- 1 (8 ounce) block cream cheddar
- 1 egg yolk

- 1/3 cup confectioners turn
- 1 tablespoon lemon juice
- 1 teaspoon lemon zing, firmly stuffed
- 1 teaspoon vanilla concentrate

Coconut Crumble Topping

- 2 tablespoons spread
- 1/4 cup almond flour
- 1/4 cup unsweetened coconut pieces
- 1 tablespoons turn sugar

Directions

1. To start set up the Blueberry Sauce: add blueberries, turn sugar and water. Permit mixture to stew until it turns out to be thick, roughly 10-15 minutes. Put in a safe spot.

For the Crust:

2. Preheat oven to 350 degrees.
3. Line an 8x8 dish with foil or material paper.
4. Consolidate the liquefied spread, almond flour and turn in a little bowl and press into the foil lined skillet.
5. Prebake covering for 7 minutes, it ought not to be firm marginally starting to brown around the edges.

6. Eliminate hull and permit it to cool. Try not to add the cheesecake layer while it is hot.

For the Lemon Cheesecake Layer:

7. Using an electric blender or little blender joins the cream cheddar, egg yolk, sugar and lemon squeeze, zing and concentrate until smooth.
8. Spread the cheesecake layer equally preposterous.

For the Blueberry Layer:

9. Spread the readied low carb blueberry sauce over the cheesecake blend.

For the Crumble:

10. Consolidate the margarine, almond flour, unsweetened coconut and sugar in a little blender or food processor and heartbeat until it takes after a piece like moisture.
11. Sprinkle over the blueberry layer.
12. Heat 18-20 minutes until the top is delicately browned.

12. Keto Cheesy Vegetable Bake

Preparation Time: 5 mins |Cooking Time: 50 mins |Total Time: 55 mins | Course: savory portions: 8

INGREDIENTS:

- 1 kg cauliflower broccoli, or any combination of vegetables of your choice (cauliflower, broccoli, zucchini, bell pepper, pumpkin, eggplant, mushrooms, [spinach, kale, asparagus - cook for 10 minutes only])
- 200 cheddar or prepared pizza cheese from 'Making it Simple' If using only mozzarella, add 1/2 teaspoon extra salt
- 4 tsp. Dijon mustard
- 500 sour cream
- 1/4 teaspoon of salt

DIRECTIONS:

1. Coarsely chop the vegetables and put them in the large Varoma steamer bowl
2. Put 500 g of water in the mixing bowl
3. Place varoma and steam 30 minutes / varoma temp / speed 3
4. Carefully remove the lid and make sure all vegetables are cooked, otherwise you have 5 minutes / VAROMA temp / speed 3 cooking
5. Remove the lid and set the varoma aside on a tea towel or on the sink to allow the steam and condensation to evaporate
6. Pour water from the mixer
7. Without washing the mixer, chop cheddar for 5 seconds / speed 5 / mc or use pizza cheese mix from 'Making it Simple'
8. Add Dijon mustard and sour cream, mix 5 seconds / speed 3 / mc
9. Pour the cooked vegetables into a large oven dish, pour over the cheese sauce and roughly stir through the vegetables
10. Bake uncovered at 180 ° C for 20-25 minutes or until golden brown

13. Keto Green Veggie Skillet

Preparation Time: 5 mins |Cooking Time: 10 mins |Ready In: 15 mins

INGREDIENTS:

- Zucchini
- 12 ounces
- (340 g)
- Olive oil
- 1 tablespoon
- (14 g or 0.49 oz.)
- salt
- ¼ tsp.
- (2 g or 0.07 oz.)
- Black pepper, ground
- ¼ tsp.
- Garlic powder

- ¼ tsp.
- Onions powder
- ¼ tsp.
- Thyme, dried
- 1 tsp.
- Butter, unsalted
- 1 tablespoon
- (14 g or 0.49 oz.)
- Spinach
- 3 ounces
- (85 g)

DIRECTIONS:

1. Cut your zucchini into quarters. Toss the pieces in a bowl with the olive oil and all the spices. Pour the contents into a saucepan over medium heat and cook, stirring occasionally, until the zucchini is soft and lightly browned.

2. Lower the heat on your stove and melt the butter in the pan. When all of the zucchini is covered, add the chopped spinach to the zucchini. Stir slowly while the spinach softens and mix in the pan. Cook the spinach to your liking - as wilted or fresh as you like!

14. Easy Keto Brownies

CAL / SERV: 260YIELD: 16 SERVINGS PREP
TIME: 0 HOURS 15 MIN
TOTAL TIME: 1 HOUR 25 MIN

INGREDIENTS:

- 4 large eggs
- 2 ripe avocados
- 1/2 c. (1 stick) melted butter
- 6 tbsp. unsweetened peanut butter
- 2 teaspoons. baking powder
- 2/3 c. Keto-friendly granulated sugar (such as Swerve)
- 2/3 c. unsweetened cocoa powder
- 2 teaspoons. pure vanilla extract
- 1/2 tsp. kosher salt
- Flaky sea salt (optional)

DIRECTIONS

1. Preheat the oven to 350 ° and line a 20 x 20 cm square pan with baking paper. In a blender or food processor, combine all *INGREDIENTS:* except flaky sea salt and blend until smooth.

2. Transfer the batter to the prepared baking pan and smooth the top with a spatula. Sprinkle with flakes of sea salt, if using.

3. Bake for 25 to 30 minutes until the brownies feel soft but not wet at all.

4. Let cool for 25 to 30 minutes before slicing and serving.

15. Keto double chocolate muffins

CAL / SERV: 280YIELD: 1 BOXES

PREPARATION TIME: 0 HOURS 10 MIN TOTAL

TIME: 0 HOURS 25 MIN

INGREDIENTS:

- 2 c. almond flour
- 3/4 c. unsweetened cocoa powder
- 1/4 c. swerve sweetener
- 1 1/2 tsp. baking powder
- 1 tsp. kosher salt
- 1 c. (2 sticks) butter, melted
- 3 large eggs
- 1 tsp. pure vanilla extract
- 1 c. sugar-free dark chocolate chips, like Lily's

DIRECTIONS

1. Preheat the oven to 350 ° and line a muffin tin with lining. In a large bowl, combine almond flour, cocoa powder, Swerve, baking powder and salt. Add melted butter, eggs and vanilla and stir until combined.
2. Fold in chocolate chips.
3. Divide batter among muffin liners and bake until toothpick inserted in center comes out clean, 12 minutes.

16. Cookie Dough Keto Fat Bombs

CAL / SERV: 70 | YIELD: 30| PREP TIME:
0 HOURS 5 MIN | TOTAL TIME: 1 HOUR 5 MIN
INGREDIENTS:

- 1/2 c. (1 stick) butter, softened
- 1/3 c. Keto-friendly confectioner's sugar (such as Swerve)
- 1/2 tsp. pure vanilla extract
- 1/2 tsp. kosher salt
- 2 c. almond flour

DIRECTIONS

1. In a large bowl with a hand mixer, beat the butter until light and fluffy. Add sugar, vanilla and salt and beat until combined.

2. Stir in the almond flour slowly until there are no more dry spots and add the chocolate chips. Cover the bowl with plastic wrap and place in the refrigerator to set, 15 to 20 minutes.

3. Use a small cookie scoop to scoop the dough into small balls. Store in the refrigerator if you plan to eat within a week, or in the freezer for up to 1 month.

17. Keto Classic Cinnamon Rolls Cinnabon

INGREDIENTS

- 1 1/2 skewers (12 tablespoons), not listed, softened, more for eating
- 1/3 cup granulated sugar
- 2-possible ground cinnamon
- All-purpose flour for pollinating
- 1-batch like Sweet-Roll Dough, follow up below
- 1 1/4 cups confectioners' sugar
- 4-tablespoons unsalted butter, melted
- 3-tablespoons of milk
- 1/2 teaspoon vanilla extract

- Pinch of salt
- 1/2 cup whole milk
- 1 1/4 packet active dry yeast (2 1/4 teaspoons)
- 1/4 liter of sugar
- 4-tablespoon are unmatched butter, melted, and slithly chilled, plis more for brusing
- 1-large yolk
- 1 1/2 vanilla extract
- 2 3/4 provides all the flour, plus more for it
- 3/4 seasoning salt
- 1/2 teaspoon freshly grated nutmeg (optional)

DIRECTIONS

1. Make the buns: A 9 to 13-inch baking dish. Watch the word and find out in a bowl. On a smooth surface, roll the dough straight out in a 10-by-18-of-inch rectach. Cut the back of the dough, leaving a 1-ish edge on one of the long pieces. Join in with the cinnamon sugar. Fizzy the rest with water. Tight job in an 18-year-old, rolling to the clean border; squeeze the signal to see.

2. Slide an elongated taut piece of thread or unflavored dental floss under the roll about 1 inch from the end. Lift the ends of the wire and move across the roll, pulling firmly to cut a piece. Repeat, cutting every 1-half-inch to make 12 rolls. Place the sandwiches in the organized baking dish.

3. Usually, treat the results with a quick wring and let them go up through heat that doubles in about 1 hour and 10 minutes.

4. Preheat the oven to 350 degrees F. Uncover the buns and bake until they pop down while pressed, 25 to 30 minutes. Only leave in the pan for 10 minutes. (You can release the baked rolls for up to 2 weeks. Be sure to cool before serving.)

5. Make the icing: while you see the item just found, it will be thick, thin, thick, and in a bowl as little as possible. Drizzle over the fun and cozy roles.

6. Heat half a cup of water and milk in a saucepan over low heat until a thermometer registers one hundred degrees F to one hundred and ten degrees F. set aside, undisturbed, until me, about 5 minutes.

7. Beat the mixed butter, add some and vanilla in the single combination until combined. In a large bowl, add the flour, sugar, egg, and nutmeg.

2. Make a well in the center, then upload the yeast combination and stir with a wooden spoon to get an idea and beat a bit. Put out a blotchy surface and knead it until slightly and elastic, about 6 minutes. Form into a ball.

3. Brush a large bowl with butter. Add the dough and turn it gently with the butter. Cover with plastic wrap and let rise at room temperature until the mixture has doubled in about 1 hour and 15 minutes.

4. Change the pot's work and flash briefly to the last examples; resume a ball and go back to the ball. At least, but a lot of the first time writing and leaving it on the dough floor. Cover the container and plastic wrap and store in the refrigerator for at least 4 hours or completely in the refrigerator.

18. Keto Homemade Glazed Donuts

INGREDIENTS

- 2-packs of 1/4 ounce packets are not single or (4½ teaspoons) yeast
- 1/3 cup of warm water 105-115F / 40-46C
- 1 1/2 cups of milk (whole milk or low-fat milk)
- 1/2 cup granulated sugar
- 1-repetition
- 2 GREATER PROPERTIES
- 1/3 cup (75 grams) butter or shortening, sometimes
- 5-cups of flour
- Canola oil for from
- ½ cup butter melted
- 2-cups powdered sugar

- 2-teaspoons of vanilla
- 5-7 tablespoons evaporated milk

DIRECTIONS

1. A stop mixer, combine lukewarm water and yeast. Don't let it appear for about 5 minutes.
2. Meanwhile, heat the milk in a microwave-safe medium bowl for about 2 minutes. Remove and let cool.
3. Add sugar, egg, eggs, or take a recipe and 2-pieces of flour to make your own.
2. Min for two minutes a month. Add the last three cups of flour and keep well. Scraping down says.
3. Place the dough in a large greased bowl. Cover loosely with a smooth cloth and allow about 1 to 2 hours of upward thrust in a warm, draft-free area until double.
4. Roll out the dough on a floured floor to about 1/4-inch thickness. Cut into donuts using a donut cutter or cookie-cutter about one inch and one inch. Let stand for about 10 minutes.
5. In a large saucepan, pour vegetable oil until it is at least 3 inches (or about five centimeters)

high and close to medium heat until the oil reaches 375.

6. I get confused once, just a few times at a time. Each time it turns over, it will take about 3 minutes, or it will turn brown. Drain on papared paper towels.

7. The bowl melts apart in a microwave oven.

8. Stay and start in one of the previous types of sugar and vanilla until everything comes together

9. Then milk evaporated (or underwater) until you reach the desired consistency

10. Dip the donuts in icing and let them drain on the rack.

19. Keto Healthy Peach Cobbler

Prep Time: 15 minutes | Cook Time: 1 hour 15 minutes | Refrigerate crust: 30 minutes | Total Time2 hours | Servings: 6 | Calories: 547kcal

Ingredients

- Covering
- 4 cups whitened almond flour
- 1/2 teaspoon salt
- 1/2 cup sugar or sugar
- 2 eggs
- 6 tablespoons unsalted margarine softened
- Peach Filling
- 1/2 cup unsalted margarine 1 stick
- 1/2 cup brown sugar or light brown sugar
- 1/2 cup sugar or sugar

- 1 teaspoon cinnamon
- 1/2 teaspoon nutmeg
- 1/2 new lemon, juice of About 2-3 tablespoons.
- 2 teaspoons vanilla Pure concentrate, not impersonation.
- 20 oz. frozen peaches This is typically 1 enormous pack. Or then again you can join various. See notes for canned or new peaches.
- 1 teaspoon cornstarch For sans gluten, use without gluten flour.
- 1 teaspoon water
- 1 egg Beaten with 1 teaspoon of water for egg wash
- cinnamon for fixing

Directions

1. Outside
2. Add the almond flour, sugar, and salt (dry ingredients) to a blending bowl. Mix to consolidate.
3. Add the eggs and dissolved spread (wet ingredients) to a different bowl and mix.
4. Add the dry ingredients to a food processor. Then, pour in the wet ingredients. Physically

beat until the blend is fused. You can likewise consolidate the dry and wet ingredients in a blending bowl and blend by hand, however subsequent to testing; the best outcomes are using a food processor.

5. Eliminate the mixture and fold it up into an enormous ball. Cut the batter fifty-fifty. One half will be utilized for the base outside of the shoemaker.

6. Sprinkle a level surface with a little almond flour to keep the batter from staying. Utilize a carrying pin and carry out the mixture until level.

7. Refrigerate the batter for 30 minutes to expedite prior to dealing with. It will be truly tacky in the event that you skirt this progression. The more you refrigerate, the simpler it is to deal with. I refrigerate half of the batter after it has been carried out, my inclination. You can keep it in a ball on the off chance that you wish.

8. After you have refrigerated, cut portion of the batter into strips around 1 inch thick.

Filling

9. Preheat oven to 350 degrees.

10. Heat a pot or pot on medium heat and add the spread. At the point when liquefied, include the sugars, nutmeg, and cinnamon. Mix constantly. Permit the combination to cook until the sugar or sugar has softened.

11. Include the lemon juice and vanilla and mix. Pour in the peaches. Mix and permit the combination to cook for around 4-5 minutes to mollify the peaches.

12. Consolidate the cornstarch and water in a little bowl to make slurry. Mix it together and add it to the pot. Mix to completely consolidate. Permit the blend to cook for 10-12 minutes until the filling thickens and eliminate it from heat.

Amass and Bake

13. Splash an 8×8 preparing dish or a 9.5 inch pie skillet with cooking shower or oil.

14. Spot 1/2 of the pie outside layer into the lower part of an 8×8 heating dish.

15. Using an opened spoon, top the outside with the peaches combination. You need to utilize

an opened spoon here with the goal that you don't add an excess of fluid to the shoemaker. On the off chance that you utilize an excessive amount of fluid it will be runny. I add it using an opened spoon, and afterward I finish it off with one huge spoonful of fluid from the pot.

16. Add cuts of pie covering to the top. You can organize the outside anyway you wish. In the event that you have lopsided strips, you can shape two together to frame one. Remove the rest of any strips that are excessively long. Brush the covering with the egg wash and sprinkle with cinnamon.

17. Heat for 25 minutes. Now the covering will start to brown. Open the oven and tent the dish with foil. Don't completely cover, freely tent (it shouldn't contact the shoemaker). This will keep the shoemaker from browning a lot on the top as the inside keeps on heating.

18. Prepare for an extra 20-25 minutes. You can eliminate the foil following 15 minutes if the covering needs seriously browning.

Important notes for recipe:

19. You can join the pie hull ingredients by hand. It will take somewhat more and can be hard to join the ingredients to deliver a smooth covering. I discover this way works best.

20. You can substitute brown sugar or sugar for white and utilize possibly white sugar in the event that you wish.

21. Loads of individuals make peach shoemaker with a top outside layer as it were. I'm a gigantic aficionado of the outside so I do both a base and top layer. You can slice the hull formula down the middle and do 1 layer in the event that you wish.

22. In the event that you lessen the measure of covering utilized in this formula (and utilize 1/2 as the top layer in particular) it will bring about the accompanying macros per serving: 251 calories, 20 grams fat, 9 grams of net carbs, and 7 grams of protein.

23. Or then again you can get serious about the top layer of the outside. This will make it simpler to make a thick cross section design in the event that you are searching for that.

24. While setting the covering into the lower part of the preparing dish, I like to utilize the lower part of a glass mug to straighten it out.

25. In the event that using canned peaches I suggest 20-24oz. At times you can just discover canned in 15.5oz servings. For this situation you may select to utilize a can and a half or go with fewer peaches. In the case of using canned, channel 1/2 of the fluid from the can prior to adding it to the pot. In the event that you utilize the entirety of the fluid the filling will turn out to be excessively soupy.

26. In the case of using new peaches, you should strip the peaches first. You may likewise need to adapt to taste. New peaches are frequently tarter and less sweet. Taste your filling over and again and add more sugar if vital.

27. In the event that you utilize locally acquired pie outside and customary sugar, the macros per serving are as per the following: 889 calories, 61 grams fat, 62 grams of net carbs, and 16 grams of protein.

28. There's an enormous contrast in insight regarding vanilla concentrate versus impersonation. Vanilla will taste much better.

29. On the off chance that you utilize locally acquired pie outside layer, the heat time will be reliable. You presumably will not have to tent the skillet with foil. Utilize your judgment. In the event that the outside begins to become a brilliant shade of brown inside 30 minutes, tent it.

30. This formula incorporates margarine. You can choose if the utilization of spread is sound or not for you. You can take a stab at using oils like coconut or avocado oil in the event that you wish.

20. Keto beef and broccoli

Preparation time: 10min | Cooking time: 25 minutes | Total time: 35 minutes | Number of meals: Calories: 294 kcal

Ingredients

1- pound steak, sliced 1/4 inch thick

5 cups of baby broccoli florets are about 7 ounces

1 tablespoon avocado oil

To prepare the sauce:

1 yellow onion, sliced

1 tablespoon butter

Half a spoonful of olive oil

1 / 3 cup of low - sodium soy sauce

- ½ cup beef broth

1 tablespoon of finely chopped fresh ginger

2 cloves of garlic, finely chopped

Instructions

Heat avocado oil in a skillet over medium heat for a few minutes or until warm. Add beef strips and cook until brown, under 5 minutes, do not stir too much, as they want to brown. Put it on a plate and set aside. Add onions to a frying pan with butter and olive oil and cook for 20 minutes until the onions are caramelized and soft.

Add all of the other sauce ingredients to the skillet and stir together over a medium heat until they begin to boil for about 5 minutes. Use a hand mixer to mix the sauce. Keep the sauce warm over low heat and add broccoli to the skillet.

Return the meat to the skillet and sauté the broccoli and sauce. Stir until covered with sauce. Bring to a boil and cook for a few more minutes until broccoli is soft. Season with salt and pepper if needed.

Serve immediately, perhaps with boiled cauliflower rice.

21. Creamy Tuscan Garlic Chicken

PREP TIME: 10 MINUTES | COOK TIME: 15 MINUTES | TOTAL TIME: 25 MINUTES | 6 SERVINGS

INGREDIENTS

- 1½ pounds boneless skinless chicken breasts daintily cut
- 2 Tablespoons olive oil
- 1 cup hefty cream
- 1/2 cup chicken stock
- 1 teaspoon garlic powder
- 1 teaspoon Italian flavoring
- 1/2 cup parmesan cheddar
- 1 cup spinach chopped
- 1/2 cup sun dried tomatoes

Directions

1. In a large skillet add olive oil and cook the chicken on medium high heat for 3-5 minutes on each side or until brown on each side and cooked until not, at this point pink in focus. Eliminate chicken and put to the side on a plate.

2. Add the substantial cream, chicken stock, garlic powder, Italian flavoring, and parmesan cheddar. Race over medium high heat until it begins to thicken. Add the spinach and sundried tomatoes and let it stew until the spinach begins to shrink. Add the chicken back to the container and serve over pasta whenever wanted.

22. Low-Carb Keto Eggplant Moussaka Recipe

Prep Time: 10 Min | Cook Time: 1 Hr. | Total Time: 1 Hr. 10 Min

INGREDIENTS

- 2 eggplants — sliced into 1/2 cm rounds
- 3 tbsp. olive oil
- 1 1/2 lb. lean ground beef or meatloaf mix
- 1 onion — small, chopped
- 2 cloves garlic — pressed
- 1 cup tomato sauce
- 1/2 cup vegetable or beef stock — could substitute with dry white wine
- 3 tbsp. parsley — chopped, fresh
- 3 tbsp. breadcrumbs — crushed pork rinds for Keto
- 2 egg whites

- 1 tsp. salt
- 1/2 tsp. black pepper
- Topping:
- 3 tbsp. butter
- 1 tbsp. cornstarch — see notes for Keto, do not use
- 1 1/2 cups milk — see notes for Keto, use 1 cup heavy cream
- 1/8 tsp. ground nutmeg
- 1 1/2 cups grated mozzarella cheese
- US Customary - Metric

INSTRUCTIONS

1. Preheat oven to 375F. Spread the eggplant rounds over one or two roasting pans. Brush with olive oil. Bake for 10 minutes, until softened and slightly dried. Let them cool.

2. In the meantime, prepare the meat sauce. Heat the remaining olive oil in a skillet, add the meat and cook until the meat is no longer pink and gets crumby. Add the onion and garlic. Cook on medium for 5 minutes.

3. Add the tomato sauce and stock (or wine). Season with salt and pepper. Bring to a boil and reduce the heat to low. Simmer for 15

minutes. Remove from heat and let the sauce cool for 10 minutes. Mix in the breadcrumbs (pork rinds for Keto) and egg whites. Add parsley.

4. Grease a 9x13 -inch baking dish (or any dish closer to these dimensions). Layer 1/2 of the eggplant rounds. Add the meat sauce. Top with the remaining eggplant rounds.

For the topping (non Keto):

5. Mix butter, milk and cornstarch in a pan. Bring to a boil, beat constantly until the mixture thickens. Lower the heat and simmer for 2 minutes. Stir in 1/2 of the cheese. Add nutmeg, 1/8 tsp. black pepper and 1/2 tsp. salt. Pour over the dish, top with the rest of the cheese and bake for 40-50 minutes at 350 F until golden.

For the topping (Keto):

6. Heat heavy cream, then add butter and 1 cup of the cheese, stir until molten. Add salt, pepper to taste and nutmeg. Pour on top of the dish, drizzle with the remaining cheese. Bake for 40-50 min at 350 F until golden.

23. Keto fried bacon omelet

Preparation Time: 5 Min | Cooking Time: 20 Min | Portions 2

INGREDIENTS:

- 4 eggs
- 5 oz. bacon cut into cubes
- 3 oz. butter
- 2 ounces fresh spinach
- 1 tablespoon finely chopped fresh chives (optional)
- Salt and pepper

DIRECTIONS:

1. Preheat the oven to 400 ° F (200 ° C). Grease an individual baking dish with butter.

2. Fry bacon and spinach in the remaining butter.

3. Beat the eggs until frothy. Mix in the spinach and bacon, including the fat leftover from frying. Add some finely chopped chives. Season with Salt and Pepper.

4. Pour the egg mixture into the baking dish (s) and bake for 20 minutes or until firm and golden brown.

5. Let cool for a few minutes and serve.

24. Keto chicken wings with creamy broccoli

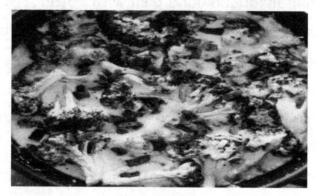

Preparation Time: 10 Min | Cooking Time: 45 Min | Portions 2

INGREDIENTS:

- Fried chicken wings
- ½ orange, juice, and zest
- ¼ cup of olive oil
- 2 tsp. ginger powder
- 1 teaspoon of salt
- ¼ tsp. cayenne pepper
- 3 lbs. chicken wings
- Creamy broccoli
- 1½ pounds of broccoli
- 1 cup of mayonnaise
- ¼ cup of chopped fresh dill
- Salt and pepper, to taste

DIRECTIONS:

1. Preheat the oven to 400 ° F (200 ° C). In a small bowl, mix juice and zest of the orange with oil and spices. Place the chicken wings in a plastic bag and add the marinade. Shake the bag well to cover the wings well.

2. Set aside to marinate for at least 5 minutes, but preferably longer. Place the wings in one layer in a greased baking dish or on a grill rack for extra crunchiness.

3. Bake on the middle rack in the oven for about 45 minutes or until the wings are golden and well cooked. In the meantime, divide the broccoli into small florets and boil them in salted water for a few minutes.

4. They should only soften a little but do not lose their shape or color. Strain the broccoli and let some of the steam evaporate before adding the remaining ingredients. Serve the broccoli with the fried wings.

25. Keto Stir-fried chicken

INGREDIENTS:

- 75 g chicken
- 1 clove of garlic
- ½ cup of bamboo shoots
- 1 tablespoon of butter
- 1 tablespoon of olive oil
- 1 dried red chili
- Chives
- Salt and pepper

DIRECTIONS:

1. Heat olive oil in a frying pan. Add the garlic and cook until it turns brown. Add the dried red chili and bamboo shoots and cook for about 3 minutes. Add the chicken, salt, and pepper. Stir and cook until the chicken is about 7 minutes. Toss in the chives and cook for 2 more minutes. Add the butter and let it sizzle for 1 minute. Place the chicken and bamboo shoots.

26. Grilled Salmon With Broccoli

INGREDIENTS:

- 100 g salmon fillet
- ½ cup of broccoli
- 2 teaspoons of butter
- ½ teaspoon of dried rosemary
- ½ teaspoon of dried thyme
- ½ teaspoon of garlic oil
- 2 tablespoons of mayonnaise with chili oil
- Salt and pepper

DIRECTIONS:

1. Mix 1 dried rosemary, dried thyme, and 1 teaspoon of butter, garlic oil, salt, and pepper in a bowl. Rub it over the salmon fillet. Preheat the grill and grill the salmon and broccoli for 6-7 minutes. Add 1 teaspoon of butter to the salmon. Sprinkle the broccoli with salt and pepper. Serve the grilled salmon and broccoli with mayonnaise-chili oil dip.

27. Grilled Flank Steak with Lemon Herb Sauce

Prep: 1 Hour 30 Min | Cooking: 30 Min | Total: 2 Hours | Servings 6

INGREDIENTS:

- 1½ pounds of flank steak
- ⅓ cup of olive oil
- ¼ cup of Worcestershire sauce
- ¼ cup of malt vinegar
- 3-cloves of garlic smashed
- 2-teaspoons chili powder
- 1-tablespoon of dried herbs (such as tarragon, thyme, or oregano, or a combination)
- Salt and freshly ground black pepper
- LEMON HERB SAUCE
- ⅓ cup of olive oil
- 3-anchovies, crushed into a paste
- 1-clove of garlic, finely chopped

- 1-tablespoon of whole-grain mustard
- 2-lemons, grated and squeezed
- ¾ cup of chopped fresh parsley
- ½ cup of freshly chopped basil
- ¼ cup of chopped fresh mint
- Salt and freshly ground black pepper

DIRECTIONS:

1. PREPARE THE STEAK: Place the flank steak in a large plastic zip-lock bag. In a medium bowl, whisk the oil with the Worcestershire sauce, vinegar, garlic, chili powder, and spices to combine. Pour the mixture over the steak and seal the bag. Marinate, chilled, for up to 1 hour.

2. MAKE THE SAUCE DURING THE STEAK MARINATES: Beat together the oil with the anchovies, garlic, mustard, lemon zest, and lemon juice. Stir in the herbs and season with salt and pepper.

3. When the steak is done marinating, remove it from the bag and wipe off the excess marinade—season with salt and pepper.

4. GRILL THE STEAK: Cook the steak on a hot grill (or grill pan) until well browned on the outside and at the desired doneness, about 5 to 7 minutes per side for medium-rare.

5. Remove the steak from the grill and let rest for 15 minutes. Slice the steak and serve immediately with the sauce.

28. Best Keto Moussaka

Prep Time: 30 minutes | Cook Time: 1 hour |
Total Time: 1 hour 30 minutes

Ingredients

For the eggplant

- 650 g eggplant 0.5 cm thick slices, no need to peel (can sub for zucchini, follow same instructions)
- 1 tablespoon salt
- 4 tablespoons olive oil

For the mince sauce

- 20 g ginger or 1/4 tsp. powder
- 10 g garlic
- 120 g celery
- 300 g onion
- 1 Tabs 20g olive oil

- 1 kg mince meat lamb, beef, pork or a combination
- 200 g cauliflower
- 250 g zucchini great way to use up some cores
- 120 g tomato paste
- 2 tsp. salt
- 1 tsp. cinnamon powder
- 2 tsp. ground allspice
- 2 tsp. dried oregano or 1 tbs fresh chopped
- For the cheese sauce
- 230 g tasty or cheddar cheese
- 500 g sour cream

Instructions

1. Firstly slice your eggplant approx. 0.5cm thick then sprinkle with salt, set aside for 10 minutes then rinse and pat dry
2. If you are happy to make more dishes, start step 5 in a pot while waiting for your eggplant
3. In your pan or skillet, on medium high heat, pan fry the eggplant slices with olive oil in consignments (don't add all the olive oil at once or your first slices will drink it all up) until well golden and softened

4. Endure until all eggplant is cooked (this is the slowest part of the recipe and can be prepared in advance). Set aside.

5. Into the same pan add the 1 Tabs olive oil and heat to medium.

6. Place ginger and garlic into the blender; chop 2 seconds / speed 7 / mc on

7. Add celery, chop 3 seconds / speed 7 / mc on

8. Add onion, chop 3 seconds / speed 5 / mc on, add to the hot pan and cook until starting to brown

9. Add the mince meat and continue to cook, stirring consistently until just starting to brown

10. In the mixer, chop cauliflower and zucchini 5 seconds / speed 4 / mc on

11. Add to the pan along with the tomato paste, spices, herbs, and salt

12. Stir through and cook on medium less heat for 30 minutes, stirring occasionally

13. Heat oven to 180C (200 if not fan forced)

14. Without washing the mixer, chop the cheese 15 seconds / speed 5 / mc on

15. Add the sour cream and stir 10 seconds / speed 4 / mc on

16. Then into a large baking dish, spread half the meat sauce, and then lay half the eggplant on top. Repeat with remaining meat then eggplant
17. Pour the cheese sauce on top and spread out evenly
18. Bake until golden, roughly 25 minutes but times will vary for different ovens
19. Serve with a side green salad drowned in extra virgin olive oil

29. Keto Beef Shawarma Bowl

YIELDS: 4 SERVINGS.

THE PREPARATION

Shawarma Beef

- 1 ½ pounds 80/20 ground beef
- 1 tablespoon garlic powder
- 1 tablespoon onion powder
- ½ tablespoon cumin
- ½ tablespoon five spice powder
- ½ tablespoon cayenne pepper
- 1 teaspoon salt
- ½ teaspoon ground black pepper
- 2 tablespoons Greek yogurt
- 2 tablespoons fresh squeezed lemon juice
- 2 tablespoons butter
- Cauliflower Rice

- 455 grams (approx. 16 oz.) cauliflower rice
- 2 tablespoons light soy sauce

White Garlic Sauce

- 2 tablespoons garlic powder
- ½ teaspoon onion powder
- 4 tablespoons Greek yogurt
- ½ teaspoon salt
- ½ teaspoon ground black pepper
- 2 tablespoons water

Red Pepper Sauce

- 1 teaspoon crushed red pepper flakes
- 1 tablespoon sriracha
- 1 tablespoon chili oil
- 2 tablespoons Greek yogurt
- ½ teaspoon salt
- ½ teaspoon ground black pepper
- Optional toppings include finely sliced cabbage, cucumber, tomatoes, avocado, etc.

The Execution

1. In a bowl, combine the ground beef and shawarma beef spices.
2. In a separate container, combine yogurt and lemon juice. Mix until consistent.
3. Combine beef and yogurt mixture. Combine well until combined and sticky. Set aside in the refrigerator while preparing the sauces.
4. For the white garlic sauce, combine all ingredients in a container. Beat to combine. Add more (or less) water for desired consistency. Transfer to a squeeze bottle or small mason jar. May be refrigerated up to two weeks.
5. Mix together all of the ingredients for the red pepper sauce. Add more (or less) water for desired consistency. Transfer to a squeeze bottle or small mason jar. May be refrigerated up to two weeks.
6. Heat 2 tablespoons of butter in a pan. Add marinated ground beef and sauté until cooked through. Transfer to a bowl and cover with foil to keep hot.

7. Meanwhile, using the same pan used to cook the beef, add cauliflower rice. Combine in the soy sauce. Keep stirring until almost dry.

8. To accumulate, layer cauliflower rice, beef, toppings, and sauces.

30. Keto crab meat and egg plate

Preparation Time: 5 Min | Cooking Time: 10 Min | Portions 2

INGREDIENTS:

- 4 eggs
- 12 oz. canned crabmeat
- 2 avocados
- ½ cup of cottage cheese
- ½ cup of mayonnaise
- 1½ oz. baby spinach
- 2 tbsp. olive oil
- ½ tsp. chili flakes (optional)
- Salt and pepper

DIRECTIONS:

1. Start cooking the eggs. Gently lower them into boiling water and let them cook for 4-8 minutes, depending on whether you want them soft or hard-boiled. Chill the eggs in ice-cold water for 1-2 minutes when cooked; this makes it easier to remove the shell. Peel the eggs.

2. Place the eggs, crab, avocado, curd cheese, mayonnaise and spinach on a plate.

3. Drizzle olive oil over the spinach. Season with salt and pepper. Sprinkle optional chili flakes over the avocado and serve.

31. Keto Chicken Sodles With Tomatoes & Spiced Cashews

Preparation Time: 5 Min | Cooking Time: 15 Min | Portions 2

INGREDIENTS:

- ½ tsp. coconut butter
- 1 medium diced onion
- 450-500 g chicken fillet
- 1 chopped garlic
- Two medium-sized courgettes
- 400 g of crushed tomatoes
- 7-10 cherry tomatoes (half cut)
- 100 g raw cashew nuts * (for spices: turmeric, paprika, and salt)
- For herbs: salt, pepper, dry oregano & basil

DIRECTIONS:

1. Heat a large pan over medium/high heat. Add coconut butter and diced onions. Cook for 30 seconds to 1 minute. Be careful not to burn the onions. Cut the chicken into 2 cm pieces.

2. Add chicken and chopped garlic to a pan. Season with basil, oregano salt, and pepper. Fry the chicken for 5-6 minutes or until golden brown.

3. While the chicken is cooking, spiral the zucchini. Cut them shorter if necessary. If you don't have a special spiralizer, just use your vegetable peeler and make zucchini ribbons. Add crushed tomatoes and simmer for 3-5 minutes. Roast the cashews in another pan (or oven) until golden brown. Season with paprika, turmeric, and salt.

4. Finally add spiral Zoodles, cherry tomatoes, and season with additional salt if needed. Cook for 1 more minute and then turn off the heat. Serve the chicken zoodles with spiced cashews and fresh basil. To enjoy!

32. Creamy Tuscan Garlic Chicken

Preparation Time: 10 Min | Cooking Time: 15 Min | Portions 6

INGREDIENTS:

- pounds skinless chicken breasts, thinly sliced
- tablespoons of olive oil
- 0.83 cup of heavy cream
- 0.42 cup of chicken stock
- 0.83 teaspoon of garlic powder
- 0.83 teaspoon of Italian herbs
- 0.42 cup of parmesan cheese
- 0.83 cup spinach chopped
- 0.42 cup of sun-dried tomatoes

DIRECTIONS:

1. Add in a large frying pan olive oil and fry the chicken over medium heat for 3-5 minutes on each side or until browned on each side and cook until no longer pink in the middle. Remove the chicken and set aside on a plate.

2. Add the whipped cream, chicken stock, garlic powder, Italian herbs, and Parmesan cheese. Beat over medium heat until it starts to thicken.

3. Add the spinach and sun-dried tomatoes and let it simmer until the spinach starts to wilt. Add the chicken back to the pan and serve over pasta if desired.

33. Rich Chocolate Glaze Keto Donuts

Prep Time: 15 min | Cook Time: 15 min | Rest time: 50 min | Total Time: 30 min

INGREDIENTS

Doughnuts:

- Nonstick oil for container
- 4 large eggs
- ½ cup unsalted margarine liquefied (112 grams)
- 3 tablespoons entire milk
- 1 teaspoon stevia glycerite (approaches ⅓ cup sugar)
- ¼ cup coconut flour
- ¼ cup unsweetened common cocoa powder (not treated with alkali)

- ¼ teaspoon ocean salt
- ¼ teaspoon preparing pop

Coating:

- ¾ cup dull chocolate chips (4.5 oz.)
- 1 tablespoon avocado oil

Guidelines

1. Preheat oven to 350 degrees F. Oil 10 silicone doughnut container depressions.
2. Whisk together the eggs, liquefied margarine, milk and stevia.
3. Speed in the coconut flour, cocoa powder, salt and heating pop.
4. Fill the doughnut skillet depressions ¾ full. Heat until set and a toothpick embedded in doughnuts confesses all, around 17 minutes.
5. Spot the container on a cooling rack and permit to cool for 15 minutes.
6. In the mean time, in a shallow bowl, soften the chocolate contributes the microwave, in 30-second spans, blending after every meeting. Mix in the avocado oil.
7. Tenderly run a blade around the edges and focus of every doughnut. Cautiously discharge

the doughnuts from the container. Plunge every doughnut into the frosting.

8. Whenever wanted, sprinkle the doughnuts with garnishes like shredded coconut or chopped nuts, or shower with softened peanut butter.

34. Keto Meatloaf

Servings: 8 Slices | Prep Time: 10 Min | Cook Time: 1 Hr. 5 Min | total Time: 1 Hr. 15 Min

INGREDIENTS

- 2 pounds 80/20 Ground beef
- 1 medium Onion, diced
- 2 cups Crushed Pork rinds
- 1 large Egg
- 2 tablespoons Worcestershire sauce
- ½ teaspoon Garlic powder
- 1 teaspoon Salt
- ⅓ cup Reduced sugar ketchup

INSTRUCTIONS

1. Preheat oven to 350 degrees F.

2. In a large bowl mix all the ingredients except ketchup. Mix ingredients until fully combined.

3. Press ingredients into a parchment paper lined loaf pan.

4. Then bake for 30 minutes. After 30 minutes add ketchup on top and bake for 25-35 minutes more.

5. Remove from oven and let rest for 15 minutes.

6. Enjoy!

NOTES

7. Net Carbs = 3g per serving

8. You can standby 1 teaspoon of onion powder for the diced onions if you'd prefer.

35. Low-Carb 30-Minute Greek Herbed Lamb

Prep Time: 15 minutes | Cook Time: 15 minutes | Total Time: 30 minutes | Servings: 4 | Calories714.5kcal

Ingredients

Lamb

- lb. lamb tenderloin (fillet)
- 1 tbsp. extra virgin olive oil
- 1 lemon, juiced (2 tbsp.)
- 1/4 tsp. pepper
- 2 tsp. dried oregano
- 1 tsp. dried parsley
- 2-3 crushed garlic cloves

Cauliflower Mash

- 2 lb. cauliflower chopped
- 1 cup light single, pouring cream
- 3 cups chicken broth
- 1 oz. unsalted butter chopped
- Himalayan salt

Instructions

1. Make mash: pour cream and chicken stock into a saucepan and turn on the heat. Break the florets off the cauliflower and chop roughly in half, add to the pan.
2. Then bring to the boil then lower the heat and simmer, covered for 15 mins.
3. Once cauliflower is simmering, make the lamb marinade.
4. Lamb marinade: Mix all the ingredients except the lamb in a small jug and mix to combine.
5. Place lamb in a zip-lock bag and pour over the marinade. Close the bag and wobble the lamb around so it's well coated. Place to marinate for about 10 minutes.
6. Put a fry-pan over medium-high heat and add 1 tbsp. olive oil.

7. Pan-fry the lamb for 3-4 minutes on each side. Rest for a few minutes if time allows.

8. While the lamb is cooking, sewer cauliflower which should be tender by now, reserving 1/4 cup of liquid.

9. Use a food processor or immersion blender to blend the cauliflower, butter, salt and the reserved liquid until pureed.

10. Present the Mediterranean lamb with the cauliflower mash.

36. Keto Corned Beef & Cabbage

YIELDS: 6 SERVINGS| PREP TIME: 0 HOURS 15 MINS | TOTAL TIME: 5 HOURS 0 MINS

INGREDIENTS

- 3-4 lbs. corned hamburger
- 2 onions, quartered
- 4 celery stems, quartered transversely
- 1 bundle pickling flavors
- Genuine salt
- Dark pepper
- 1 medium green cabbage, cut into 2" wedges
- 2 carrots, stripped and cut into 2" pieces
- 1/2 c. Dijon mustard
- 2 tbsp. apple juice vinegar
- 1/4 c. mayonnaise

- 2 tbsp. escapades, generally chopped, in addition to 1 tsp. saline solution
- 2 tbsp. parsley, generally chopped

DIRECTIONS

1. Spot corned hamburger, onion, celery, and pickling flavors into a large pot. Add sufficient water to cover by 2", season with salt and pepper, and heat to the point of boiling. Lessen heat to low, cover, and stew until delicate, 3–3 1/2 hours.

2. In the mean time, whisk Dijon mustard and apple juice vinegar in a little bowl and season with salt and pepper. In another bowl, blend mayo, tricks, escapade salt water, and parsley. Season with salt and pepper

3. Add cabbage and carrots and keep on stewing for 45 minutes to 1 hour more, until cabbage is delicate. Eliminate meat, cabbage, and carrots from pot. Cut corned meat and season with more salt and pepper.

4. Present with the two sauces as an afterthought for plunging.

37. Keto Rosemary & Olive Focaccia Bread

Prep Time: 15 Minutes | Cooking Time: 25 Minutes |Total Time: 40 Minutes | Servings: 10 Servings | Calories: 284kcal

INGREDIENTS:

- 4 ounces of cream cheese softened
- 4 ounces of salted butter softened
- 4-large eggs
- 1 3/4 cups of almond flour
- 1-teaspoon of baking powder
- 1/4 teaspoon xanthan gum
- 1/2 teaspoon garlic powder
- 3-sprigs of rosemary
- 16 kalamata olives

DIRECTIONS:

1. Preheat your oven to 190C / 375F and line an 8x12in a baking pan with parchment paper. Place the cream cheese and butter in a mixing bowl and beat with your hand mixers at high speed until fluffy. Add the eggs one at a time and beat well. Don't worry if the mixture looks curdled; it will come together when the dry is added. Add the almond flour, baking powder, xantham gum, and garlic powder and mix well. Once combined, swap the hand mixer for a spatula and mix well. Spoon the mixture onto the baking tray and smooth it out. Finish with the olives and rosemary. Place in the oven and bake for 18-25 minutes; the focaccia is cooked when it springs back to the touch. Enjoy warm or cool and slice to use for sandwiches.

Conclusion

I would like to thank you for choosing this book. All the recipes in this book are very beneficial for carb lovers and tastes like more carb meals. These recipes are more delicious and rich in nutrients. You must try at home and appreciate.

I wish you all good luck!

CPSIA information can be obtained
at www.ICGtesting.com
Printed in the USA
LVHW011706160521
687588LV00002B/196